STRAIGHT FORWARD

MATH SERIES
ADVANCED
BOOK 1

PRE-ALGEBRA

by S. Harold Collins

Book design by Kathy Kifer

Published by:
Garlic Press
100 Hillview Lane #2
Eugene, OR 97401

ISBN 0-931993-28-8
Order Number GP-028

To Parents and Teachers:

The Pre-Algebra Book 1 and Pre-Algebra Book 2 are part of our **Advanced Straight Forward Math Series**. They are designed for parents and teachers of children.

These Pre-Algebra books will help parents and teachers direct children in the transition from basic mathematics to algebra. These two books are a natural extension of our Straight Forward Math series and Advanced Straight Forward Math Series which have presented the basic and advanced mathematical operations of addition, subtraction, multiplication, and division.

Pre-Algebra Book 1 and 2 provide the mathematical skills needed by students to succeed in algebra groupings. Abstractions are kept to a minimum. Each pre-algebra topic includes an explanation and multiple exercises to reinforce the explanation presented.

Two measurement tools are provided. A Beginning Assessment Test will survey a student's beginning skill pre-algebra level. A Post Assessment Test will measure how well the pre-algebra skills have been mastered.

Exercises can be completed in the book or on separate paper. Answers to exercises are provided. And the Beginning Assessment Test and Post Assessment Test have been arranged according to pre-algebra topics.

CONTENTS

Beginning Assessment Test

Factors: Circle the numbers that are factors of the first number.

1. 6 : 1 2 3 4   **4.** 20 : 2 8 10 15

2. 8 : 2 4 6 9   **5.** 15 : 2 3 5 9

3. 19 : 5 9 10 19   **6.** 22 : 2 3 4 9

Prime number is a number that is divisible by itself and 1 only

Prime/Composite: Are the following numbers prime (mark **P**) or composite (mark **C**)?

1. 3 P   **4.** 50 C   **7.** 93

2. 4 C   **5.** 76 C   **8.** 79

3. 5 P   **6.** 29 P   **9.** 37

Exponent/Powers: Write the following as products of prime numbers.

1. 2^2 = 4 = 2×2   **4.** 6^3 =216 (2×3)(2×3)(2×3)
(3×3)(3×3) (3×3)(3+3) (3×3)(3+3) 6^3 = 6×6×6 =216 =

3. 9^4 9×9×9×9=56   **5.** 4^3 64
4×4×4=64 = (2×2)(2×2)(2×2)

6. 10^2 **6.** 7^5
10×10 = 100 = 2×50 = 2×2×25 = 2×2×5×5   (7×7)(7×7)(7

GCF: Find the Greatest Common Factor for each set of numbers.

Greatest Common Factor is the biggest number that multiplies into both numbers

1. 3 , 8   3→1,3   GCF=1   **3.** 12 , 18   18 1,2,3,6,9,18
8→1,2,4,8   12 1,2,3,4,6,12   GCF=6

2. 10 , 15   **4.** 9 , 15   9 1,3,9   GCF=3
10 - 1,2,5,10 GCF=5   15-1,3,5,15
15 - 1,3,5,15

continued

1

LCM: Find the Lowest Common Multiple for each set of numbers.

Lowest common multiple is the lowest number that both these numbers are a factor of.

1. 2 , 6 $2 \times 3 = 6$ $LCM = 6$ **3.** 7 , 6
    $1 \times 6 = 6$

$7 - 7, 14, 21, 28$ $LCM = 2$ 72

$LCM = 42$

2. 8 , 12 $24 = 8$ **4.** 8 , 9

$8 = 0, 8, 16, 24, 32 \ldots$ $LCM = 12$
$12 = 0, 12, 24, 36 \ldots$

8	16	24	32	40	48	56	72
9	18	27	36	45	54	63	72

Ratio: Change each of the following to a fraction.

1. 3 out of 4 $\dfrac{3}{4}$

3. 5 quarts to 9 quarts $\dfrac{5}{9}$

2. 7 out of 10 people $\dfrac{7}{10}$

4. 29 out of 35 children $\dfrac{29}{35}$

Proportion: Place an **=** or an **≠** between these proportions.

1. $\dfrac{21}{7} = \dfrac{3}{1}$ (÷7, ÷7)

3. $\dfrac{2}{3} \neq \dfrac{12}{19}$ (×6, ×6 = 18)

2. $\dfrac{4}{5} = \dfrac{12}{15}$ (×3, ×3)

4. $\dfrac{5}{1} \neq \dfrac{5}{10}$

Percent: Complete each column. Reduce when necessary.

Percent	Fraction	Decimal
1.	$\dfrac{41}{100}$	.41
2. 40%		.4
3. 250%	$2\dfrac{1}{2}$	

Factors

If two or more numbers are multiplied, then each number is
a **factor** of the product.

Listing all the ways to express a number as a product yields
all factors of that number.

Example 1:   For the number **24,** there are these different sets of factors:

$$1 \times 24 \quad = 24$$
$$2 \times 12 \quad = 24$$
$$3 \times 8 \quad = 24$$
$$4 \times 6 \quad = 24$$

We can say, the whole number factors of **24** are: **1, 2, 3, 4, 6, 8, 12, 24.**

Example 2:   Is **12** a factor of **60** ?
It is if 12 divides evenly into 60.
$$60 \div 12 = 5.$$
12 divides evenly into 60.
It divides evenly 5 times.
Both **5** and **12** are factors of **60**.

Example 3:   Is **25** a factor of **60** ?
It is if 25 divides evenly into 60.
$$60 \div 25 \quad \text{does not give an even answer.}$$
25 is not a factor of **60**.

Factor Exercise 1: State (yes or no) whether 10 is a factor for each of the following.

1. 10   **2.** 42   **3.** 700   **4.** 925

5. 580   **6.** 1,120   **7.** 3,242   **8.** 17,433

9. 320   **10.** 1,100   **11.** 800   **12.** 7,921

13. 10,300   **14.** 42,501   **15.** 7,000   **16.** 90   continued

Factors

Factor Exercise 2: Find all possible sets of factors for each number.

1. 2   **2.** 3   **3.** 10   **4.** 12

5. 17   **6.** 18   **7.** 21   **8.** 24

9. 50   **10.** 36   **11.** 27   **12.** 45

13. 55   **14.** 60   **15.** 40   **16.** 26

Factor Exercise 3.: Circle the numbers that are factors of the first number.

1. 6 : 1   2   3   4   **2.** 14 : 5   6   7   8   **3.** 15 : 2   3   5   9

4. 19 : 5   9   10   19   **5.** 27 : 3   6   9   12   **6.** 32 : 2   3   5   8

7. 37 : 5   7   6   8   **8.** 8 : 2   4   6   9   **9.** 35 : 3   5   7   9

10. 20 : 2   8   10   15   **11.** 28 : 4   8   12   16   **12.** 45 : 3   6   9   12

13. 30 : 3   5   12   20   **14.** 16 : 2   4   6   8   **15.** 22 : 2   3   5   9

Factor Exercise 4: Answer yes or no.

1. Is 7 a factor of 63?   **2.** Is 5 a factor of 32?   **3.** Is 12 a factor of 12?

4. Is 3 a factor of 117?   **5.** Is 4 a factor of 46?   **6.** Is 3 a factor of 19?

7. Is 24 a factor of 144?   **8.** Is 1 a factor of 13?   **9.** Is 10 a factor of 190?

continued

Divisibility

Divisibility Tests are short cuts for finding factors of whole numbers.

Here are four useful divisibility tests:

1. A number is divisible by **2** if the last digit is an even number. **0, 2 , 4, 6, 8.**

2. A number is divisible by **3** if the digits add up to **3**, **6**, or **9**.

   Examples: $411 = 4 + 1 + 1 = 6$

   $9,855 = 9 + 8 + 5 + 5 = 27 \qquad 2 + 7 = 9$

3. A number is divisible by **5** if the last digit is **0** or **5**.

4. A number is divisible by **10** if the last digit is **0**.

Divisibility Exercise 1: State (yes or no) whether each number is divisible by 2.

1. 91	**2.** 36	**3.** 67
4. 15	**5.** 112	**6.** 389
7. 1,000	**8.** 12,567	**9.** 486
10. 12,010	**11.** 7,784	**12.** 18,001

Divisibility Exercise 2: State (yes or no) whether each number is divisible by 3.

1. 51	**2.** 36	**3.** 82
4. 75	**5.** 198	**6.** 617
7. 402	**8.** 2,382	**9.** 6,253
10. 51,790	**11.** 42,127	**12.** 111,111

continued

Divisibility

Divisiblity Exercise 3: Write 5 or 10 beside each number that can be divided by 5 or 10.

1. 40

2. 52

3. 515

4. 901

5. 682

6. 1,215

7. 3,400

8. 850

9. 972

10. 89,760

11. 8,927

12. 112,001

Divisiblity Exercise 4: Using your knowledge of divisibility, state if the following problems can be divided by 2, 3, 5, or 10.

1. 84

2. 77

3. 55

4. 147

5. 792

6. 150

7. 291

8. 135

9. 123

10. 1,300

11. 2,382

12. 960

13. 414

14. 101

15. 880

Prime & Composite Numbers

Prime Numbers: A whole number greater than 1 that has only 1 and itself as factors.

Composite Numbers: A whole number greater than 1 that has at least one factor besides itself and 1.

Prime Factorization: Every composite number can be expressed as a product of only prime numbers.

Examples: **6**   **12**   **100**   **100**

$$2 \times 3 \qquad 3 \times 4 \qquad 10 \times 10 \qquad 4 \times 25$$

$$3 \quad 2 \times 2 \qquad 2 \times 5 \quad 2 \times 5 \qquad 2 \times 2 \quad 5 \times 5$$

Prime/Composite Exercise 1: Circle all prime numbers. Cross out all composite numbers.

$$
\begin{array}{cccccc}
1 & 2 & 3 & 4 & 5 & 6 \\
7 & 8 & 9 & 10 & 11 & 12 \\
13 & 14 & 15 & 16 & 17 & 18 \\
19 & 20 & 21 & 22 & 23 & 24 \\
25 & 26 & 27 & 28 & 29 & 30 \\
\end{array}
$$

Prime/Composite Exercise 2: Use your knowledge of divisibility to tell whether each number is a composite (mark **C**) or a prime (mark **P**).

1. 17   **2.** 37   **3.** 45   **4.** 10

5. 41   **6.** 50   **7.** 131   **8.** 44

9. 81   **10.** 79   **11.** 65   **12.** 82

13. 53   **14.** 76   **15.** 93   **16.** 67

continued

Prime and Composite Numbers

Prime/Composite Exercise 3: Write each composite number as a product of only prime numbers.

1. $18 = 2 \times 3 \times 3$ 2. 27   3. 12

4. 39   5. 125   6. 48

7. 144   8. 88   9. 46

10. 64   11. 81   12. 20

13. 225   14. 49   15. 65

16. 450   17. 35   18. 91

Prime/Composite Exercise 4: Find 2 prime numbers (without using 1) whose sum is the given number for each of the following.

1. $8 = 3 + 5$ 2. 6   3. 22   4. 18

5. 10   6. 20   7. 90   8. 16

9. 14   10. 24   11. 12   12. 76

Prime/Composite Exercise 5: Give the least prime number (other than 1) that will divide each of the following.

1. 12 ; 2   2. 55   3. 21   4. 49

5. 81   6. 44   7. 35   8. 77

9. 63   10. 62   11. 121   12. 169

Prime/Composite Exercise 6: Give the greatest prime number (other than 1) that will divide each of the following.

1. 14 ; 7   2. 84   3. 70   4. 65

5. 30   6. 12   7. 48   8. 51

9. 16   10. 33   11. 49   12. 121

Exponents & Powers

3^2 The number **3** is a base number.

The number **2** is an exponent.

The exponent is the number of times the base is used as a factor.

3 is a factor **2** times, or **3** x **3**. The product is the composite number **9**. $3^2 = 9$.

Power is a number that can be written using an **exponent**.

4^2 = **4** to the second power, or **4** x **4**.

3^3 = **3** to the third power, or **3** x **3** x **3**.

2^4 = **2** to the fourth power, or **2** x **2** x **2** x **2**.

Power/Exponent Exercise 1: Name the base and the exponent for the following.

1. 3^4	**2.** 2^5	**3.** 1^6
4. 100^2	**5.** 7^6	**6.** 6^2
7. 12^3	**8.** 10^4	**9.** 3^{10}

Power/Exponent Exercise 2: Show the following as the product of prime factors.

1. 2^2	**2.** 10^3	**3.** 5^3
4. 9^4	**5.** 6^5	**6.** 7^4
7. 13^2	**8.** 3^6	**9.** 1^4

continued

Exponents and Powers

Power/Exponent Exercise 3: Write each of the following using exponents.

1. $1 \times 1 \times 1 \times 1$ **2.** 10×10

3. $5 \times 5 \times 5$ **4.** 12×12

5. $7 \times 7 \times 7 \times 7$ **6.** $19 \times 19 \times 19$

7. $5 \times 5 \times 5 \times 5 \times 5$ **8.** $6 \times 6 \times 6$

9. $11 \times 11 \times 11$ **10.** 12 to the fifth power

11. 10 to the sixth power   **12.** 6 squared

Power/Exponent Exercise 4: Find the value of each expression.

1. 2^2 **2.** 3^3 **3.** 4^2

4. 2^5 **5.** 1^8 **6.** 7^2

7. 5^3 **8.** 2^4 **9.** 4^3

10. 10^3 **11.** 9^3 **12.** 11^2

13. 6^4 **14.** 20^3 **15.** 18^1

Greatest Common Factors

The **Greatest Common Factor (GCF)** of two numbers is the greatest (largest) number that is a factor of each number.

There are two methods to find the **GCF**:

Method 1: •List all factors of each particular number.
•List all factors in common.
•The largest common factor will be the **GCF**.

Example 1:

12   18

Factors of 12= 1, 2, 3, 4, 6, 12
Factors of 18= 1, 2, 3, 6, 9, 18

Common factors are 1, 2, 3, and 6

The **GCF = 6**
6 is the largest factor both have in common.

Example 2:

9   15

Factors of 9= 1, 3, 9
Factors of 15= 1, 3, 5, 15

Common factors are 1 and 3

The **GCF = 3**
3 is the largest factor both have in common.

Method 2: •Reduce the number to prime factors using prime factorization.
•List all of the prime factors the numbers have in common.
•Multiply the common prime numbers together to get the **GCF**.

continued

Example 3:

$$36 \qquad 24$$

$$36 = 6 \times 6 = 3 \times 2 \times 3 \times 2$$
$$24 = 3 \times 8 = 3 \times 2 \times 2 \times 2$$

Common factors are $2 \times 2 \times 3$ or $2^2 \times 3$
The **GCF** $= 2^2 \times 3 =$ **12**

12 is the product of common factors

Example 4:

$$60 \qquad 30 \qquad 90$$

$$60 = 6 \times 10 = 3 \times 2 \times 2 \times 5$$
$$30 = 3 \times 10 = 3 \times 2 \times 5$$
$$90 = 3 \times 30 = 3 \times 3 \times 10 = 3 \times 3 \times 2 \times 5$$

Common factors are $2 \times 3 \times 5$
The **GCF** = **30**

30 is the product of the common factors.

GCF Exercise 1: Give all the common prime factors each pair of numbers share.

1. $4 = 2 \times 2$
$6 = 2 \times 3$

2. $8 = 2 \times 2 \times 2$
$12 = 2 \times 2 \times 3$

3. $21 = 3 \times 7$
$42 = 3 \times 7 \times 2$

4. $27 = 3 \times 3 \times 3$
$36 = 3 \times 3 \times 2 \times 2$

5. $56 = 2^3 \times 7$
$84 = 2^2 \times 3 \times 7$

6. $24 = 2 \times 2 \times 2 \times 3$
$16 = 2 \times 2 \times 2 \times 2$

7. $125 = 5^3$
$25 = 5^2$

8. $64 = 2 \times 2 \times 2 \times 2 \times 2 \times 2$
$80 = 2 \times 2 \times 2 \times 2 \times 5$

9. $28 = 2 \times 2 \times 7$
$34 = 2 \times 17$

GCF Exercise 2: Find the GCF for each set of numbers.

1. 3 , 8

2. 18 , 21

3. 6 , 36

4. 12 , 30

5. 20 , 35

6. 24 , 40

7. 36 , 45

8. 13 , 15

9. 48 , 96

10. 21 , 28

11. 64 , 40

12. 30 , 50

13. 100 , 500

14. 19 , 57

15. 140 , 40

16. 16 , 42

17. 10 , 15 , 25

18. 8 , 10 , 15

19. 12 , 18, 24

20. 6 , 8 , 4

continued

Greatest Common Factors

GCF, Exercise 3: What is the GCF for each set of number?

1. $2 = 2$
$4 = 2 \times 2$

2. $4 = 2 \times 2$
$12 = 2 \times 2 \times 3$

3. $9 = 3 \times 3$
$18 = 3 \times 3 \times 2$

4. $6 = 2 \times 3$
$18 = 3 \times 3 \times 2$

5. $5 = 5$
$7 = 7$

6. $10 = 2 \times 5$
$20 = 2 \times 2 \times 5$

7. $12 = 2 \times 2 \times 3$
$18 = 3 \times 3 \times 2$

8. $55 = 5 \times 11$
$99 = 3 \times 3 \times 11$

9. $15 = 3 \times 5$
$18 = 2 \times 3^2$

10. $27 = 3^3$
$39 = 3 \times 13$

11. $28 = 2^2 \times 7$
$25 = 5^2$

12. $9 = 3^2$
$27 = 3^3$

13. $28 = 2^2 \times 7$
$52 = 2^2 \times 13$

14. $30 = 3 \times 2 \times 5$
$50 = 5 \times 5 \times 2$

15. $24 = 2^2 \times 6$
$66 = 6 \times 11$

16. $4 = 2^2$
$8 = 2^3$
$24 = 2^3 \times 3$

17. $15 = 3 \times 5$
$35 = 7 \times 5$
$60 = 2^2 \times 3 \times 5$

18. $27 = 3^3$
$54 = 2 \times 3^3$
$72 = 2^3 \times 3^2$

19. $24 = 2^3 \times 3$
$36 = 2^2 \times 3^2$
$48 = 2^4 \times 3$

20. $9 = 9$
$27 = 3^3$
$81 = 3^4$

GCF Exercise 4: Find the GCF for each set of numbers.

1. 40 , 60

2. 99 , 66

3. 10 , 12

4. 40 , 24

5. 24 , 66

6. 18 , 11

7. 56 , 16

8. 34 , 85

9. 90 , 126

10. 108 , 144

11. 42 , 116

12. 6 , 8 , 12

13. 4 , 8 , 24

14. 36 , 48 , 56

15. 30 , 48 , 120

16. 33 , 42 , 90

17. 27 , 54 , 108

18. 24 , 36 , 48

19. 50 , 78 , 112

20. 100 , 50 , 25

Least Common Multiples

The **Least Common Multiple (LCM)** of two or more numbers is the least number that each has as a factor, except zero.

Another way of stating **LCM** is: It is the first number (except zero) that can be divided evenly by any compared set of numbers.

There are two methods you can use to find the LCM.

Method 1: • List multiples
 • Identify the first number (multiple) that each has in common.

Example 1:   **3   5**
Multiples of 3 are: 0 , 3 , 6 , 9 , 12 , 15 , 18
Multiples of 5 are: 0 , 5 , 10 , 15 , 20
LCM = 15

Example 2:   **4   6   8**
Multiples of 4 are: 0 , 4 , 8 , 12 , 16 , 20 , 24
Multiples of 6 are: 0 , 6 , 12 , 18 , 24 , 30
Multiples of 8 are: 0 , 8 , 16 , 24 , 30
LCM = 24

Method 2: • Reduce number to prime factors.
 • Select the greatest powers that each factor has in common.
 • Multiply all common greatest powers.

Example 1:   **12   16**
Prime factors of 12 are: $2 \times 2 \times 3$
$$2^2 \times 3$$
Prime factors of 16 are: $2 \times 2 \times 2 \times 2$
$$2^4$$
The greatest powers of all factors are: 3 and 2^4
LCM $= 3 \times 2^4 =$ **48**

Example 2:   **18   27   30**
$18 = 3 \times 3 \times 2 = 2 \times 3^2$
$27 = 3 \times 3 \times 3 = 3^3$
$30 = 2 \times 3 \times 5 = 2 \times 3 \times 5$
The greatest powers of all factors are: $2 \times 3^3 \times 5$
LCM $= 2 \times 3^3 \times 5 =$ **270**

continued

14

Least Common Multiples

LCM Exercise 1: List the multiples. Find the LCM.

1. 2 , 6

2 =

6 =

LCM =

2. 9 , 12

9 =

12 =

LCM =

3. 8 , 12

8 =

12 =

LCM =

4. 2 , 10

2 =

10 =

LCM =

5. 3 , 4

3 =

4 =

LCM =

6. 6 , 4

6 =

4 =

LCM =

7. 5 , 6

5 =

6 =

LCM =

8. 2 , 8

2 =

8 =

LCM =

9. 7 , 6

7 =

6 =

LCM =

10. 6 , 8

6 =

8 =

LCM =

11. 4 , 7

4 =

7 =

LCM =

12. 4 , 9

4 =

9 =

LCM =

LCM Exercise 2: Find the LCM.

1. 5 , 6

5 =

6 =

LCM =

2. 5 , 7

5 =

7 =

LCM =

3. 8 , 9

8 =

9 =

LCM =

4. 10 , 14

10 =

14 =

LCM =

continued

Least Common Multiples

5. 8 , 12

8 =

12 =

LCM =

6. 15 , 8

15 =

8 =

LCM =

7. 18 , 32

18 =

32 =

LCM =

8. 12 , 16

12 =

16 =

LCM =

9. 14 , 21

14 =

21 =

LCM =

10. 15 , 75

15 =

75 =

LCM =

11. 4 , 8 , 12

4 =

8 =

12 =

LCM =

12. 9 , 12 , 15

9 =

12 =

15 =

LCM =

LCM Exercise 3: Use multiples to find LCM.

1. 3 , 4 , 6

3 =

4 =

6 =

LCM =

2. 7 , 21 , 84

7 =

21 =

84 =

LCM =

3. 10 , 12 , 15

10 =

12 =

15 =

LCM =

4. 6 , 8 , 12

5. 4 , 5 , 8

6. 4 , 8 , 16

continued

Least Common Multiples

7. 30 , 15 , 75

8. 6 , 50 , 100

9. 6 , 9 , 18

10. 7 , 21 , 84

11. 6 , 9 , 12

12. 15 , 36 , 75

Ratios, Proportions & Percents

A **ratio** is a comparison of two numbers by division.

A ratio can be written in several ways:

$$3 \text{ to } 4 \qquad 3:4 \qquad \frac{3}{4}$$

Advertisements are a common source of ratios:

"3 out of 4 doctors prefer....."	3 to 4	3 : 4	$\frac{3}{4}$
"9 out of 10 people agree....."	9 to 10	9 : 10	$\frac{9}{10}$
"2 out of 3 products contain....."	2 to 3	2 : 3	$\frac{2}{3}$

In mathematics, we usually write a ratio as a fraction. Some fractions can be simplified. The ratio in an advertisement which states, "75 out of 100 people prefer Brand X", can be simplified as follows:

$$\frac{75}{100} = \frac{3}{4} \qquad \text{The GCF of } 75 \text{ and } 100 \text{ is } 25.$$

In other words, we can reduce ratios to lowest terms without changing the relationships of the numbers being compared. They are still equivalent.

We can also change ratios by multiplication and they will stay equivalent. As long as both numerators and denominators are multiplied by the same number (but not zero), they will remain equivalent.

Ratios Exercise 1: Change each of the following to a fraction:

1. 3 out of 7 people

2. 5 cups to 9 cups

3. 27 out of 33 people

4. 1 out of 2 free throws

5. 3 miles in 5 hours

6. 53 pennies out of 97 coins

continued

Ratios

Ratio Exercise 2: Equivalent ratios. Tell what number replaces the question mark.

1. $\frac{1}{2} = \frac{1 \times ?}{2 \quad 10}$

2. $\frac{3}{4} = \frac{3 \times 5}{4 \times ?}$

3. $\frac{7}{8} = \frac{7 \times 3}{? \times 3}$

4. $\frac{2}{3} = \frac{? \times 4}{3 \times 4}$

5. $\frac{6}{12} = \frac{6 \div 6}{12 \div ?}$

6. $\frac{3}{15} = \frac{3 \div ?}{15 \div 3}$

7. $\frac{175}{250} = \frac{? \div 25}{250 \div 25}$

8. $\frac{28}{56} = \frac{28 \div 28}{? \div 28}$

9. $\frac{14}{16} = \frac{14 \div ?}{? \div 2}$

Ratio Exercise 3: Give two equivalent ratios for each of the following.

1. $\frac{1}{4}$

2. $\frac{2}{3}$

3. $\frac{25}{50}$

4. $\frac{70}{100}$

5. $\frac{7}{9}$

6. $\frac{2}{17}$

7. $\frac{2}{5}$

8. $\frac{7}{16}$

9. $\frac{21}{27}$

10. $\frac{3}{4}$

11. $\frac{15}{20}$

12. $\frac{5}{7}$

Ratio Exercise 4: Change each ratio to lowest terms. Express as a fraction.

1. 2 to 6

2. 3 out of 15

3. 14 : 24

4. 8 to 6

5. 11 out of 121

6. 16 : 4

7. 5 out of 15

8. 8 to 10

9. $\frac{13}{52}$

10. $\frac{18}{81}$

11. $\frac{30}{50}$

12. $\frac{24}{9}$

Ratio Exercise 5: Compare each pair of ratios. Place an = sign or an ≠ sign between pairs.

1. $\frac{2}{4}$ $\frac{4}{8}$

2. $\frac{8}{9}$ $\frac{88}{99}$

3. $\frac{3}{8}$ $\frac{15}{40}$

4. $\frac{14}{17}$ $\frac{7}{9}$

5. $\frac{8}{9}$ $\frac{19}{21}$

6. $\frac{32}{12}$ $\frac{8}{2}$

7. $\frac{3}{4}$ $\frac{15}{16}$

8. $\frac{33}{40}$ $\frac{165}{200}$

9. $\frac{9}{13}$ $\frac{19}{23}$

10. $\frac{5}{8}$ $\frac{15}{25}$

11. $\frac{13}{21}$ $\frac{65}{105}$

12. $\frac{8}{6}$ $\frac{26}{22}$

19

Ratios, **Proportions** & Percents

A **proportion** names two equivalent ratios.

An easy method to determine if two ratios are equivalent is by multiplying cross products.

Example 1: $\dfrac{3}{4} = \dfrac{15}{20}$ $4 \times 15 = 60$
$3 \times 20 = 60$

If the cross products are equal, the ratios are equivalent.

Example 2: $\dfrac{2}{3} \neq \dfrac{10}{16}$ $3 \times 10 = 30$
$2 \times 16 = 32$

Proportions Exercise 1: Place and **=** or an ≠ sign between these proportions.

1. $\dfrac{21}{7}$ $\dfrac{3}{1}$ 2. $\dfrac{7}{5}$ $\dfrac{25}{4}$ 3. $\dfrac{2}{3}$ $\dfrac{8}{12}$ 4. $\dfrac{6}{8}$ $\dfrac{2}{3}$

5. $\dfrac{30}{45}$ $\dfrac{6}{9}$ 6. $\dfrac{6}{15}$ $\dfrac{3}{7}$ 7. $\dfrac{28}{22}$ $\dfrac{8}{6}$ 8. $\dfrac{4}{5}$ $\dfrac{12}{15}$

9. $\dfrac{7}{5}$ $\dfrac{9}{3}$ 10. $\dfrac{8}{9}$ $\dfrac{16}{17}$ 11. $\dfrac{12}{8}$ $\dfrac{40}{28}$ 12. $\dfrac{2}{3}$ $\dfrac{12}{19}$

13. $\dfrac{9}{4}$ $\dfrac{54}{24}$ 14. $\dfrac{1.2}{1.6}$ $\dfrac{3}{4}$ 15. $\dfrac{3.2}{3.5}$ $\dfrac{5}{6}$ 16. $\dfrac{12}{18}$ $\dfrac{2}{3}$

17. $\dfrac{3}{8}$ $\dfrac{6}{16}$ 18. $\dfrac{4.3}{1.4}$ $\dfrac{3}{1}$ 19. $\dfrac{2.4}{32}$ $\dfrac{.75}{10}$ 20. $\dfrac{50}{9}$ $\dfrac{10}{3}$

21. $\dfrac{4}{5}$ $\dfrac{13}{15}$ 22. $\dfrac{.5}{1}$ $\dfrac{5}{10}$ 23. $\dfrac{.25}{.75}$ $\dfrac{1}{3}$ 24. $\dfrac{10}{7}$ $\dfrac{9}{6.4}$

20

Ratios, Proportions & **Percents**

A ratio that compares a number to 100 is a **percent**.
The mathematic symbol for percent is **%**.

Changing Decimals to Percents.

Move decimal points two places to the right, add a % symbol.

Example: 1

.23	= .2̣3̣.	= 23%
.75	= .7̣5̣.	= 75%
3.5	= 3 . 5̣ 0̣.	= 350%
.025	= .0̣2̣.5	= 2.5%
.205	= .2̣0̣. 5	= 20.5%

Changing Fractions to Decimals.

Change the fraction to a decimal. Move the decimal point two places to the right, add a % symbol.

Example 1:

$$\frac{15}{100} = .15 = 15\%$$

$$3\frac{27}{100} = 3.27 = 327\%$$

$$\frac{325}{1000} = .325 = 32.5\%$$

Example 2:

$$4\overline{)3.00}^{\,.75} \quad = 75\%$$

$$8\overline{)3.00}^{\,.375} \quad = 37.5\%$$

$$3\overline{)2.00}^{\,.666} \quad = 66.6\%$$

When numbers continue on, you must round off. In the last case, the answer continues on in 6's indefinitely.

continued

Percents

Percent Exercise 1: Write each decimal as a percent.

1. .75	**2.** .21	**3.** 2	**4.** .35
5. .025	**6.** 3.2	**7.** .05	**8.** .005
9. 5.5	**10.** .0125	**11.** 3.96	**12.** 10.2
13. 6.0	**14.** .451	**15.** 2.90	**16.** 6.223
17. 1.011	**18.** 17.8	**19.** .731	**20.** .1679

Percent Exercise 2: Write each percent as a decimal number.

1. 75%	**2.** $12\frac{1}{2}$%	**3.** 827%	**4.** 15.2%
5. $6\frac{1}{2}$%	**6.** $24\frac{3}{4}$%	**7.** $3\frac{7}{10}$%	**8.** $25\frac{1}{4}$%
9. 4.8%	**10.** 25.25%	**11.** $90\frac{1}{2}$%	**12.** 127.4%

Percent Exercise 3: Write each fraction as a percent.

1. $\frac{1}{10}$	**2.** $\frac{1}{2}$	**3.** $\frac{1}{4}$	**4.** $\frac{1}{8}$
5. $\frac{7}{10}$	**6.** $\frac{1}{20}$	**7.** $\frac{3}{5}$	**8.** $\frac{3}{8}$
9. $\frac{3}{4}$	**10.** $\frac{1}{50}$	**11.** $\frac{5}{100}$	**12.** $\frac{1}{5}$
13. $1\frac{5}{8}$	**14.** $4\frac{9}{20}$	**15.** $6\frac{5}{10}$	**16.** $14\frac{1}{4}$
17. $3\frac{7}{8}$	**18.** $\frac{1}{16}$	**19.** $14\frac{3}{8}$	**20.** $6\frac{7}{50}$
21. $11\frac{9}{10}$	**22.** $2\frac{27}{100}$	**23.** $\frac{4}{5}$	**24.** $5\frac{1}{2}$

continued

Percents

Percent Exercise 4: Complete each column. Reduce fraction when necessary. Round decimals to nearest hundreth when necessary.

Percent	Fraction	Decimal
1.	$\dfrac{31}{100}$	.31
2. 40%		.4
3. 92%	$\dfrac{23}{25}$	
4.	$\dfrac{7}{10}$	.7
5. 50%		.5
6.	$\dfrac{1}{8}$	.125
7. 2%	$\dfrac{1}{50}$	
8. 35%		.35
9.	$\dfrac{43}{100}$	.43
10. 7.5%	$\dfrac{3}{40}$	
11. 7%		.07
12. 30%	$\dfrac{3}{10}$	
13.	$\dfrac{1}{5}$	.2
14. 75%		.75

continued

15. $62\frac{1}{2}\%$ $\frac{5}{8}$

16. $\frac{1}{3}$ .333

17. $8\frac{3}{4}\%$ .0875

18. $1\frac{27}{100}$ 1.27

19. 71.7% $\frac{717}{1000}$

20. $\frac{21}{200}$ .105

21. 143%   1.43

22. .5% $\frac{1}{200}$

23. $\frac{2}{3}$ .667

24. 1000%   10

25. 342% $3\frac{21}{50}$

Final Assessment Test

Factors: Answer yes (**y**) or no (**n**).

1. Is 7 a factor of 63 ?

2. Is 5 a factor of 32 ?

3. Is 3 a factor of 19 ?

4. Is 4 a factor of 46 ?

5. Is 24 a factor of 144 ?

4. Is 1 a factor of 11 ?

Prime/Composite: Give only prime numbers for these composite numbers.

1. 18

2. 39

3. 64

4. 88

5. 49

6. 65

Exponents/Powers: Find the value of each expression.

1. 2^5

2. 5^3

3. 4^3

4. 9^4

5. 7^2

6. 1^7

GCF: Find the Greatest Common Factor for each set of numbers.

1. 6 , 8 , 12

2. 4 , 8 , 24

3. 24 , 36 , 48

4. 100 , 50 , 25

LCM: Find the Least Common Multiple for each set of numbers.

1. 6 , 8 , 12

2. 4 , 8 , 12

3. 4 , 8 , 16

4. 6 , 50 , 100

continued

Proportions: Place an = or an ≠ proportion.

1. $\dfrac{12}{8}$ $\dfrac{40}{28}$ 3. $\dfrac{15}{16}$ $\dfrac{3}{6}$

2. $\dfrac{2}{3}$ $\dfrac{6}{9}$ 4. $\dfrac{7}{8}$ $\dfrac{21}{24}$

Percent: Complete each column. Reduce when necessary.

Percent	Fraction	Decimal
1.	$3\dfrac{27}{100}$	3.27
2. 2.5%		.025
3. $62\dfrac{1}{2}$	$\dfrac{5}{8}$	